Valuing Quality in the Early Years

A framework for developing your current practice

Carmen Mohamed and Sarah Lissaman

Published 2009 by A & C Black Publishers Limited
36 Soho Square, London W1D 3QY
www.acblack.com

ISBN 978-1-4081-1255-7

Text © Carmen Mohamed and Sarah Lissaman

A CIP record for this publication is available from the British Library.

Printed in Great Britain by Martins the Printers Ltd

This book is produced using paper that is made from wood grown in managed, sustainable forests. It is natural, renewable and recyclable. The logging and manufacturing processes conform to the environmental regulations of the country of origin.

To see our full range of titles
visit www.acblack.com

Valuing Quality in the Early Years © Carmen Mohamed and Sarah Lissaman

Contents

About the authors

"Change is essential for us to grow but that change needs to come from within."

(Best and Thomas, 2007)

Carmen Mohamed taught in East London for ten years before moving to Leicestershire where she was Lead Foundation Stage Consultant, responsible for implementing changes towards quality Foundation Stage provision. Whilst working for Leicestershire Local Authority she wrote several practitioner publications, including guidance for anti-bias, quality development and good practice. She has been a key note speaker at both local and national conferences for Early Years practice. She is currently a Lecturer in Primary Education at the University of Leicester.

Sarah Lissaman has been involved in teaching and caring for children all her professional life, becoming a registered childminder when she took a break from teaching to bring up her own children. She currently supports the development of high quality early education across Leicestershire as an Early Learning and Childcare Improvement Advisor.

Carmen and Sarah both still work and live in Leicester, with their young families, and continue to pursue a keen interest in the education of young children through research and in supporting Early Years practitioners in developing their understanding of quality.

This book has been developed in direct response to the practitioners they work with who have requested clear guidance on how to identify how well they are doing and how they need to develop their practice next. They are grateful to their colleagues from Leicestershire, who continually help to secure their vision of high quality learning in the Early Years.

Although no document has knowingly been directly quoted, the authors have been influenced by statutory (including the EYFS) and non-statutory guidance in this field. Some terminology and principles that have become common usage may well be found within the framework. This is a result of a shared understanding of what constitutes high quality care and education for young children. The authors apologise to anyone who may feel they have been quoted; this has been unwitting on their part.

What is it all about?

This book is for all Early Years practitioners who wish to improve the quality of the provision throughout the 0-5 sector. It is a structured self-evaluation framework that offers you a set of quality criteria to benchmark your provision and give you ideas for future improvement. It will help you to identify your own next steps in progress.

The aim of the book is to help you to become even more effective at managing change and development in your setting and to help you to rediscover the joys of working with young children in order to maximise their enjoyment of learning. The book has been designed to offer you an easy to use set of quality criteria that will help you to continually improve between Ofsted inspections.

Our motivation for writing the framework was to put all our knowledge and expertise in one place for the benefit of all the practitioners we have worked with who want to aim high. We have shared with you all the best ideas of the moment, so that you can see where you are in your great aim of achieving high quality for the children in your care and to help you to see the bigger picture of what other people might be doing.

This book has been put together using the knowledge gained from years of working with Early Years practitioners who have been changing their practice regularly according to the latest government initiatives. The ideas contained within the book are the culmination of years of sharing ideas and implementing recognised good practice in a range of environments. While undertaking the writing of the book, advice was sought from current practitioners in different types of settings. It takes into account shifting government educational priorities and initiatives, and is founded on research undertaken in this field over the last decade.

One of our principles is to support you in listening to children and in taking account of how attending your setting makes them and their parents feel. This notion is taken directly from *The United Nations Conventions on the Rights of the Child*, Articles 12 and 13, and is followed up in all Ofsted inspections.

With the introduction of the Early Years Foundation Stage (EYFS), it seemed like a good time to write the valuing quality self-evaluation framework (SEF) using feedback from practising Early Years specialists. This book is aligned with current thinking and terminology and relates specifically to the new EYFS without repeating the guidance.

The framework provides criteria for Early Years settings and schools to establish where their strengths are and what they need to do next in order to improve the quality of their provision. It enables practitioners to gather evidence of good practice that can be used towards their SEF and future inspections.

The framework is aimed at all those who work with children in the Early Years to give clear guidance to settings for improvement:

- **Foundation Stage teachers**
- **Nursery and Pre-school practitioners**
- **Managers of Early Years settings and Children's Centres**
- **Childminders**
- **Local Authority advisors**.

The framework will support all those settings striving to achieve better quality provision for children. Our belief is that if you are in charge of what you want to improve and have ideas about how to improve, you are well on your way to achieving your goal.

The framework follows the *Five Outcomes for Children* laid out in the *Every Child Matters* paper and uses similar terminology to the schools' self-evaluation framework to enable all practitioners working within the EYFS to easily access the document.

The framework promotes the development of good practice with reference to *Key Elements of Effective Practice* (KEEP), showing a clear understanding of the recent changes to the British early education system.

We have used terms that relate to the school SEF (forms.ofsted.gov.uk) so that those of you who work in schools will be able to dovetail into your school's improvement programme: **Emerging, Evolving, Establishing** and **Enhancing**. We also think these are positive ways of describing your setting, especially if you are new to this field.

New ideas are continually being introduced by researchers in the field and this framework helps to put some of the latest into perspective for you. This includes ideas about how to improve *Education Outside the Classroom* and *Nurturing Creativity*.

An excellent feature is that it also ties in with Local Authorities' drive to improve quality for children within their reach.

Practitioners are able to:
- **review all areas of provision;**
- **easily assess where they are;**
- **gather examples as evidence;**
- **see what needs to be changed.**

For the purpose of this book the term 'staff' refers to anyone involved in the running of the setting, including lunchtime supervisors, cleaners, gardeners, premises officers, cooks, administrators and anyone else specific to your setting.

'Practitioners' refer to those adults involved in the care and learning of the children attending the setting.

The importance of self-evaluation

Everyone who works in Early Years education knows how important it is to evaluate provision in order to enhance the learning and development of young children. With the introduction of the Ofsted framework, there is ever growing responsibility for settings to evaluate their own provision on a regular basis.

The current system means that you need to demonstrate to inspectors that you can not only diagnose where your strengths and weaknesses are, but more crucially that you have a system for development.

Self-evaluation is central to effective practice. This framework offers a range of quality criteria for EYFS practitioners to aid self-evaluation and improvement. It will:

- help you to identify what you do well and areas that need refinement;
- encourage you to see that regular reflection that is open but critical will lead to better provision;
- enable you to take advantage of some of the latest theories about what is most effective;
- encourage you to be brave about trying out new ideas;
- provide you with a user-friendly self-evaluation tool that can be used by Early Years practitioners of any level of qualification or experience;
- offer suggestions about the evidence you may provide towards meeting the targets within each strand;
- provide a structure for your self-improvement plan, ensuring everyone is involved;
- support you in progressing a continuous cycle of review and development;
- provide an indication of progression from 'Emerging' to 'Enhancing' your practice;
- indicate how to use your findings alongside the EYFS documentation.

You are best placed to recognise your own strengths and weaknesses. This framework is useful to confirm where you are now and to provide the means to establish where you need to go to build on that good practice.

The results can be used to show how you are adding value to the children's experiences through the collation of evidence. The information is then available for appraisal or performance management meetings with staff to show how they are progressing as professionals. It can even support your own understanding of best practice to enhance your career development.

Providers of early education in all types of settings will be able to use the guidance to:
- **identify** where they can find evidence towards a given statement;
- **judge** the current quality of their provision for themselves;
- look forward to finding ways to **improve**.

Practitioners are able to review all areas of provision whatever their experience, level of qualification or the nature of their setting.

This book is aimed at all those who work in the Early Years Foundation Stage sector to give clear guidance for improvement:

- **Foundation Stage teachers** can use it alongside the school development plan to ensure consistency of provision across the school. The whole staff team should be involved in gathering evidence

- **Nursery and Pre-school practitioners** can involve the whole staff team in reflecting on progress. However, it may be the responsibility of the leader or manager to ensure rigour and consistency of evidence

- **Managers of Early Years settings** and Children's Centres can lead their team in providing evidence of successful practice across the setting through each of the rooms

- **Childminders** can use it independently or with the support of parents and are likely to share their findings as part of the network for support and for moderation purposes

- **Local Authority advisors** can use it alongside settings to agree evidence and support leaders in driving quality

We know from experience that involving **all** practitioners in the process is more likely to ensure a lasting impact. Therefore, it is a good idea to:

- use the statements for a basis of discussions at staff/team meetings and ensure that all practitioners have an input in the implementation of progress.

- ensure each member of the setting is able to share ideas about how they want to progress and therefore gain satisfaction from seeing changes put into practice.

- give everyone a chance to be part of the team and take ownership for the quality of provision to ensure continued good practice.

For each of the five key areas there are four columns (strands), which represent stages in a continuum of development and effectiveness.

It should be assumed that the progression includes and extends what is evidenced in the strand before. Each strand represents improvements in practice and provision. It does not imply a complete change in practice at each level, but gives guidance on how to build on the practice that is already in place. This way, you can go from strength to strength.

Strands

Emerging is the starting point from which you will develop the practice in your setting. It implies that you meet the minimum EYFS standards.

Evolving suggests that from the evidence you collect, you are considering how your provision is meeting the needs of the children you are working with.

Establishing shows evidence that you are beginning to reflect on how you meet the development and learning of all children in an inclusive environment.

Enhancing provides guidance for settings that continuously reflect on their provision and offer professional development opportunities to all staff who come into contact with the children. You are offering high quality learning and development opportunities.

There are no time limits to this process as these must be decided according to the developments that need to take place. Leaders and managers are advised to continuously assess the impact of the changes on the provision, environment and children as an ongoing review of the setting will ensure that progress is made and quality is assured.

Initially the framework should be used as a whole staff resource to stimulate discussion and reflection across the whole document, while working in depth on specific sections.

Remember, however small a change, as long as it shows benefits, it has to be a good thing.

1. Scan through each section of the book to familiarise yourself with the contents.
2. Decide as a team which areas you would like to develop first. The starting point can be anywhere as the framework is designed to be used in any order.
3. Read through the four strands in your chosen section – emerging, evolving, establishing and enhancing.
4. Agree which strand you are working at currently and begin to find evidence to support your claim. This is your starting point for development.
5. Begin to gather evidence of practice from your setting and put it into the appropriate strand. Evidence may span more than one strand.
6. This will identify where the gaps are and you will be able to discuss ways to improve provision in order to meet the criteria in the next strand.
7. Decide how you can make the changes and who will be responsible for which parts of the work.
8. Use the action plan at the back of the book to plan your way forward using small but achievable targets.
9. Set realistic timescales for your group with halfway points for a progress meeting.
10. Begin to put the agreed changes and developments in place.
11. Meet again at the agreed time so that you are confident that progress is being made.
12. At the final progress meeting, use the same section of the framework to review how successful you have been in changing practice and provision. Discuss any areas you have not managed to tackle as effectively as you thought you might.
13. Identify difficulties that may have occurred and agree ways to overcome any barriers. Try not to ignore difficulties – find a way to get over them.
14. When you are confident that you can see the benefits of your changes, move to another area and repeat the process again in your own time.

Be brave.

Open your mind to the possibilities of an outstanding provision.

Be willing to challenge your beliefs.

Be willing to try new approaches.

(Adapted from Best and Thomas, 2007)

Where evidence might be found

When you are looking for evidence of the impact of your setting on the children, you might look at:

- how you are **planning** the learning for the children;

- how the children access the **resources**;

- **observations** of the children involved in play activities;

- observations of the children's **interests** and learning styles;

- **assessments** of the children's learning;

- monitoring and **tracking** the children's learning;

- the children's **involvement** in planning their own learning;

- observations of **adult** interactions;

- observations of the learning **environment**;

- responses to **parent** questionnaires;

- **policies** and procedures evident in practice;

- staff **appraisals** and performance management.

This list is not exhaustive but a guide to where you can start your audit trail of evidence.

What settings might do with the outcomes

The results of the evaluation process can be used to show how you are adding value to the children's experiences through the collation of evidence. Adding value includes all the experiences offered to the children that will enhance the quality of their learning. In some instances 'value added' relates only to the attainment of a child over time. We firmly believe that we should take into account how Early Years provision supports the social, emotional and personal development of children, how much of their time they can spend outside exploring the natural environment, how much creative freedom they have and how independently they are able to guide the direction of their experiences.

The information you gather supports your own understanding of best practice, which in turn will improve your personal ability to enhance your own career development. When you find an area you would like to develop within the learning environment or practice, you will be guided to find further information to enhance your knowledge and understanding. Use the websites and books suggested at the end of this book as a starting point or look for further training in that area. Be careful not to take on too many new initiatives or you will spread yourself too thinly. Take care to select an area that all your team are keen to develop. This will make the task a very positive experience for you as well as the children.

Your reflection about new ideas and a deeper understanding of quality in the Early Years will be available for you to use in your appraisal or performance management meeting with your line manager to show how you are progressing as a professional.

Factors to evaluate	Emerging	Evolving	Establishing	Enhancing
Practitioners encourage children to form a positive attitude and disposition to learning. **EYFS themes** *Enabling Environments* *Learning and Development*	• Children feel good about their efforts and are positively encouraged to try new and different activities. • Curriculum requirements are understood and are implemented effectively.	• Children are positive about what and how they are learning. • Positive encouragement is used effectively, ensuring children try new and different activities without fear of mistakes. • Children are given the appropriate space and time they need to persevere at their activities. • Children are encouraged to plan their own activities.	• Children are positively encouraged through successful personal development. • Children feel secure in taking risks in their learning and development. • Effective questioning helps children to begin to understand what they have learnt and what they might learn next. • Children develop the essential skills to take initiative in their own learning.	• Children talk about their learning and are encouraged to set personal goals to challenges and extend themselves. • Time is allowed for sustained concentration and perseverance. • Children are equipped with the necessary skills to develop their own learning.

Evidence

How well are children helped to enjoy and achieve?

Factors to evaluate	Emerging	Evolving	Establishing	Enhancing
Practitioners effectively foster the personal development of the children to ensure they enjoy their time in the provision. **EYFS themes** *A Unique Child* *Enabling Environments* *Positive Relationships*	• Positive relationships are established with children; adults listen to them and respond appropriately. • Children trust the key person and other adults to care for their needs.	• Children are respected and there is a positive atmosphere within the setting. • Children who are finding it difficult to learn and behave appropriately are supported effectively.	• Children are listened to and feel valued by the adults. Feelings are taken seriously. • Groupings are structured to encourage more experienced children to support, talk with, share and co-operate with younger, less experienced children.	• Children know that their views will be taken into account when any decisions about them are made. • Practitioners support and extend knowledge, skills, understanding and confidence and help children to overcome any disadvantage.

Evidence

Factors to evaluate	Emerging	Evolving	Establishing	Enhancing
Practitioners understand the individual and diverse ways that children learn. **EYFS themes** *A Unique Child* *Enabling Environments* *Learning and Development*	• All children can access the activities on offer and they are allowed to make decisions about how to play. • Children are enabled to learn in different ways and at different rates. • Children who have different learning and development needs are identified and supported appropriately.	• New experiences are introduced in familiar contexts and related to children's interests and schemas. • A range of multi-sensory activities are on offer to the children at all times. • Children are helped to overcome barriers to learning through appropriate challenge and support. • Language and vocabulary that children already understand are used and extended.	• Each child's understanding is constantly monitored through questioning and encouraging children to ask questions, and by observing their body language. • Each child's preferred learning styles are supported through an appropriate balance of visual, oral, sensory and kinaesthetic provision. • The environment is organised to ensure that all children can freely access all activities.	• Personalised learning, development and care is understood and planned for by adults. • Use of all senses is recognized in planning as the most effective method of learning. • Barriers to learning and development are removed through an all-inclusive environment.

Evidence

How well are children helped to enjoy and achieve?

Factors to evaluate	Emerging	Evolving	Establishing	Enhancing
Practitioners understand that children develop rapidly and at differing rates during the Early Years. **EYFS themes** *A Unique Child* *Enabling Environments* *Learning and Development*	• Opportunities are provided for children to select preferred activities. • A range of play that allows children to practise and develop new skills is provided.	• Children who need more time to practise with a new activity are identified and provided for. • Children are encouraged to consolidate their learning over time. • Relevant and appropriate content matches differing abilities and stages of development.	• Children have space and time, and can be active in their learning. • Planning inspires and stimulates in order to secure and extend learning. • Children are told the purpose of activities and are helped to challenge themselves to extend their learning.	• Children are supported to be independent in developing their chosen learning experiences; they are helped to understand the purpose of activities and encouraged to spend time revisiting to consolidate their thinking through exploration and investigation.

Evidence

Factors to evaluate	Emerging	Evolving	Establishing	Enhancing
The curriculum is effectively structured with planned, purposeful activities that stimulate the children's enthusiasm. **EYFS themes** *Enabling Environments* *Learning and Development*	• There is a daily plan with a variety of indoor and outdoor activities for the children to choose from. • Children's choice of activities is monitored to ensure a balance across the curriculum. • Each of the six areas of learning and four themes are well documented.	• Planning refers to learning intentions and develops different aspects of learning and development. • The environment is organised to provide opportunities for a range of child-led activities. • Planned learning experiences are effectively supported outside as well as inside. • Unforeseen events are sometimes used to stimulate interest in the children.	• There are planned activities relating to children's interests, building on what children already know and can do, and challenging their thinking. • Children become involved in planning experiences that are mostly based on real-life situations, making good use of routine and unforeseen events. • Purposeful activities provide opportunities for learning both indoors and outdoors.	• Provision for different starting points from which children develop their learning, building on what they can already do, is carefully monitored. • Effective use is made of unforeseen opportunities for children's learning that arise from everyday events and routines. • The purposeful structure of the learning environment allows children to consolidate and extend their own learning.

Evidence

How well are children helped to enjoy and achieve?

Factors to evaluate	Emerging	Evolving	Establishing	Enhancing

There are opportunities for children to engage in selecting and planning their own learning experiences.
 	
EYFS themes
 	
   Enabling Environments
 	
   Learning and Development
	• Opportunities are planned for children to make their own decisions in play, including selecting resources for play.
	
	• Children have the opportunity to revisit learning experiences regularly.
		• Opportunities are provided for children to extend their own activities over several days.
		
		• Children select from a wide range of activities and resources to increase independent learning.
			• Children are encouraged to select activities and resources to follow their own learning and schemas.
			
			• Children are encouraged to learn from each other.
			
			• Resources are available that inspire children to create their own ideas and experiences.
				• Children are encouraged to make decisions about how they use their time, who they work with and the resources they use.
				
				• Children have time to become engrossed, work in depth and complete activities.

Evidence

Valuing Quality in the Early Years © Carmen Mohamed and Sarah Lissaman

Factors to evaluate	Emerging	Evolving	Establishing	Enhancing
Practitioners use their knowledge and understanding of the children to extend learning. **EYFS themes** *Positive Relationships* *Learning and Development*	• Practitioners engage with children whilst at play, spending time playing alongside children, watching and listening to their understanding and vocabulary. • Practitioners support children in making links in their learning.	• Children are encouraged to talk about their activities so that adults can find out what they know and can do, and to develop their thinking skills. • Practitioners begin to use a range of questioning techniques when supporting children's learning. • Practitioners understand how to support children in making links in their learning.	• Purposeful intervention by practitioners engages children in the learning process. • Practitioners recognise when children are deeply engaged in an activity. • Children's thinking skills are extended by encouraging them to explain their learning.	• Purposeful intervention by practitioners will challenge the children's learning. • Skilful questioning helps children to explore their own knowledge and understanding. • Through skilful questioning, adults clear misconceptions and encourage sustained shared thinking.

Evidence

How well are children helped to enjoy and achieve?

Factors to evaluate	Emerging	Evolving	Establishing	Enhancing
Practitioners ensure challenge is appropriate through effective observation. **EYFS themes** *Enabling Environments*	• Children's progress is monitored across the curriculum by key practitioners. • Key practitioners make regular observations of the children's learning and development.	• Children's progress is regularly monitored to identify next steps in learning and action is taken to provide appropriate support. • Children with different learning needs are sufficiently supported and appropriately challenged.	• Assessments are used effectively to plan next steps in learning and ensure children are making good progress. • Observations are used to identify learning priorities and plan challenging, relevant and motivating learning experiences.	• Skilful observations of children and the curriculum are used in evaluating next steps in the planning cycle. • Regular and skilful observations of each child's achievements, interests and learning needs are made.

Evidence

Factors to evaluate	Emerging	Evolving	Establishing	Enhancing
Activities promote development and use of language. **EYFS themes** *A Unique Child* *Learning and Development*	• The curriculum has a wide range of activities that encourage speaking and listening, and rhymes and stories.	• Children's vocabulary is extended as they play. • Practitioners begin to use a range of techniques when supporting children's language development, including questioning and modelling sentence construction.	• Conversation and carefully phrased questions are used to develop children's knowledge of spoken language. • Appropriate and accurate language and correct grammar is used by practitioners.	• The use of a rich vocabulary and correct grammar by all practitioners. • Skilful questioning helps children to explore their own knowledge and understanding. • Children's language skills are extended by encouraging them to explain their learning.

Evidence

How well are children helped to enjoy and achieve?

Factors to evaluate	Emerging	Evolving	Establishing	Enhancing

Practitioners have a clear understanding of how teaching and learning changes and develops as children move through the Early Years Foundation Stage.
 	
 EYFS themes
 	
   Enabling Environments
 	
   Learning and Development
	• Activities are organised and managed to ensure children can access activities by age group.
	
	 • Learning experiences are targeted for children's specific development.
		• Activities are appropriately differentiated to meet the learning needs of groups of children.
		
		 • Practitioners use their knowledge of the children to develop shared learning experiences.
			• Activities are appropriately differentiated to meet the learning needs of individual children.
			
			 • Children are encouraged to plan how to develop or extend an activity according to their own interests.
				• Differentiated activities offer challenge and support in relation to individual children's age and stage of development.
				
				 • Children are encouraged to plan activities and select their own resources to develop their own learning interests.

Evidence

Factors to evaluate	Emerging	Evolving	Establishing	Enhancing
Provision made for the children's physical development. **EYFS themes** *A Unique Child* *Learning and Development* *Enabling Environments*	• Activities are planned every session to encourage large movement inside and outside.	• Purposeful physical activities based on progression of development are planned at least once a day. • Movement is recognised as a key learning skill.	• Children choose to be inside or outside for their activities. • There is always a variety of activities available for developing a range of gross motor skills.	• Children can access outdoor provision and engage in physical activity throughout the session. • 'Forest School' or other off site specialist provision is regularly experienced.

Evidence

How well do you help children to be healthy?

Factors to evaluate	Emerging	Evolving	Establishing	Enhancing
Provision for children's social and emotional development. **EYFS themes** *A Unique Child* *Positive Relationships*	• Children are positively encouraged to make friends and share. • Children feel secure and happy in the setting.	• Children are confident to express their feelings try out new things and set their own challenges. • Their ideas are listened to, making them feel valued. • Children are helped to make decisions about changes made to their space within the setting.	• Children confidently take risks in a secure environment. • High expectations of social behaviour are required by practitioners at all times. • Children are able to cope with changes made within the setting.	• Children are confident to challenge their own learning. • Children can negotiate friendships and build positive relationships. • Children manage change with relative ease and security.

Evidence

Factors to evaluate	Emerging	Evolving	Establishing	Enhancing
Provision is made for children to eat and drink, and to learn about healthy eating. **EYFS themes** *A Unique Child* *Learning and Development*	• Children are provided with balanced meals and a time to eat healthy snacks. • Health professionals are invited into the setting to talk to the children about how to stay fit and healthy.	• Children are encouraged to enjoy different foods and understand why some foods are healthy and others are not. • Menus are produced to give parents choice and information about meals.	• Children's health is promoted by a wholesome, nutritious and well-balanced diet, including dishes from other cultures. • Meal and snack times are relaxed and social occasions are celebrated where children are taught the art of conversation.	• Children's healthy eating is promoted through a range of positive activities. • Children help with the preparation of snacks and with serving at meal times. • Children are allowed to have a snack to suit their own needs but are encouraged to enjoy the time as a social occasion.

Evidence

How well is the setting organised and managed?

Factors to evaluate	Emerging	Evolving	Establishing	Enhancing

How the physical environment supports learning and development.
 	
EYFS themes
 	
  Enabling Environments
 	
  Learning and Development
	• The environment is welcoming and friendly.
	
	• Children have space to move and be active, and are encouraged to take their learning outside regularly.
	
	• Children use easels and the floor as well as tabletops.
		• The environment is well organised so that children can select and access equipment safely.
		
		• Indoor activities are taken outside to provide a different quality and a larger space without noise restrictions.
		
		• Children use a range of different surfaces inside and outside.
			• An attractive, stimulating environment varies learning experiences for the children.
			
			• The outdoor space is effectively used as an integral part of the learning environment.
			
			• Children freely use a range of surfaces to support their own development in a purposeful manner.
				• An exciting, stimulating environment invites children to challenge and extend their learning in a variety of ways.
				
				• The outdoors provides a natural resource for holistic learning experiences.
				
				• Children are free to choose and explore a whole range of surfaces and experiences.

Evidence

Valuing Quality in the Early Years © Carmen Mohamed and Sarah Lissaman

How well are children protected from harm or neglect and helped to stay safe?

Factors to evaluate	Emerging	Evolving	Establishing	Enhancing
The quality and use of equipment enhances learning. **EYFS themes** *A Unique Child* *Enabling Environments*	• Children are supervised to use a variety of tools, some of which are real. • A variety of resources from different home situations is used in play. • Natural resources are provided for play and discussion.	• Children are supervised when using a range of real tools in real-life situations. • A range of resources from home situations and the natural world is utilised in play to enhance knowledge and vocabulary. • Children are supported in gaining the necessary knowledge and confidence to assess risks and dangers.	• Children are taught to use real tools and equipment safely and appropriately in their chosen activities. • Resources and equipment reflect real situations to enhance children's learning and development. • Children are able to assess risks and dangers in a range of situations.	• Children are provided with a wide range of appropriate tools and equipment for real-life situations. • All equipment and resources reflect real situations to enhance learning and vocabulary through multi-sensory experiences. • Children are able to calculate risks and dangers when making decisions.

Evidence

How well are children protected from harm or neglect and helped to stay safe?

Factors to evaluate	Emerging	Evolving	Establishing	Enhancing
Safety and risk assessment procedures ensure children are free from harm. **EYFS themes** *A Unique Child*	• Staff are familiar with documentation on health and safety. • There is an appointed person to do regular maintenance checks. • Children are kept safe within a secure environment.	• Staff are aware of records of regular maintenance checks on indoor and outdoor equipment. • Relevant documentation is kept in an accessible place.	• Staff make regular checks on all equipment and the environment to which the children are exposed and report any risks. • Relevant documentation is kept in an accessible place.	• Practitioners make regular checks on all equipment and the environment to which the children are exposed. Report and ensure action is taken on any risks or dangers. • Relevant documentation is kept in an accessible place.

Evidence

Factors to evaluate	Emerging	Evolving	Establishing	Enhancing
Provision for 'safeguarding children' is accounted for in an effective policy. **EYFS themes** *A Unique Child* *Positive Relationships* *Enabling Environments*	• All staff have an enhanced CRB check and have received training in appropriate Safeguarding Children procedures. • Staff are familiar with documentation and the named person for safeguarding children. • Staff, children and parents are aware of the procedures to report concerns.	• Staff understand how to observe and monitor children at risk and are sensitive and confidential with the information. • Staff, children and parents are aware of the procedures to report concerns.	• Staff understand how to observe and monitor children at risk and are sensitive and confidential with the information. • Staff, children and parents are aware of the procedures to report concerns.	• Staff understand how to observe and monitor children at risk and have a professional approach to sensitive and confidential information. • Staff, children and parents are aware of the procedures for reporting concerns.

Evidence

How well are children protected from harm or neglect and helped to stay safe?

Factors to evaluate	Emerging	Evolving	Establishing	Enhancing
The effectiveness of equality of opportunity and anti-discriminatory practice. **EYFS themes** *A Unique Child*	• Children are neither excluded nor disadvantaged because of ethnicity, home language, family background, SEN, disability, gender or ability. • Anti-bias policy and procedures are agreed and adhered to by all members of staff.	• Resources are available which reflect diversity and discourage discrimination and stereotyping. • Staff use display to reflect the cultural and ethnic diversity of society. • All team members take part in training to develop their understanding of equality issues.	• Practitioners develop children's attitudes of empathy and tolerance. • Practitioners observe the children's actions and learning with specific equality issues in mind. • Practitioners can sensitively and tactfully address discrimination in children and adults. • Materials, equipment and displays reflect the community the children come from and the wider world.	• Practitioners take an active interest in individual characteristics, backgrounds and abilities of the children. • Cultural and religious backgrounds are regarded as positive assets. • Practitioners confidently address and challenge all types of discrimination by children and adults. • Staff provide a model of good practice in their language, behaviour and attitudes.

Evidence

Factors to evaluate	Emerging	Evolving	Establishing	Enhancing
A safe and supportive learning environment is free from harassment. **EYFS themes** *Positive Relationships*	• Adults and children have positive, happy relationships. • Parents are welcomed into the setting. • Practitioners are aware of children's agencies that can support parents with children who have difficulties. • The environment supports children, parents and staff to report concerns.	• Through training and development, staff understand how to enhance their relationships with both adults and children in ways that are sensitive, positive and non-judgemental. • Practitioners know when and how to involve children's agencies that can support parents with children who have difficulties. • The environment supports children, parents and staff to report concerns.	• Children's differing realities are valued and viewed positively by the staff. • Parents are encouraged to share their knowledge of the children's home life. • Sensitive involvement of children's agencies is supportive for parents. • The environment encourages children, parents and staff to report concerns.	• Practitioners use their own learning to improve their work with young children and their families in ways that are sensitive, positive and non-judgemental. • Regular involvement with children's agencies removes barriers for parents. • The environment encourages children, parents and staff to report concerns.

Evidence

Factors to evaluate	Emerging	Evolving	Establishing	Enhancing

The effectiveness of the partnership with parents and carers in promoting children's learning.
 	
EYFS themes
   Positive Relationships
   Enabling Environments
	• Positive relationships with parents are established in order to work effectively with their children.
	
	• Parents are routinely informed about the learning and development at the setting.
		• Practitioners are informed about children's learning and development at home.
		
		• Parents have open access to information about their child's learning and development.
		
		• Practitioners help parents to recognise their importance as role models for their children.
			• Comprehensive arrangements are in place for informing parents about the progress of their child.
			
			• Parents are encouraged to recognise the educational significance of comments made by the child at home.
			
			• Parents are recognised as the main carers and their knowledge and information about their child is sought and respected.
				• Practitioners show parents that the unique knowledge they have about their child is valued in the setting.
				
				• Practitioners actively seek advice from parents about their child and issues relating to their learning and development.
				
				• Parents are encouraged to contribute to records and learning journeys.

Evidence

Factors to evaluate	Emerging	Evolving	Establishing	Enhancing

The quality of evidence of children's social and emotional competence.
 	
EYFS themes
  A Unique Child
  Enabling Environments
	• The layout of the room enables children to develop effective social skills.
	
	• Routines enable children to feel known as an individual and to develop emotional security.
	
	• Noise levels are managed to support both learning and care appropriately.
	
	• Children are supported in working together to develop friendship groups.
		• With support, children can try out new activities and more difficult learning experiences, persisting until they achieve success.
		
		• Children are enabled to recognise their feelings and supported in appropriate ways of dealing with them.
		
		• There is a calm atmosphere with consistent boundaries in which children can develop independence, self-esteem and confidence.
			• Children are able to take risks independently with new activities and more difficult learning experiences, persisting until they achieve success.
			
			• Children are engaged in decision-making activities, knowing that their ideas and concerns will be listened to.
			
			• Children are encouraged to practise social skills in real situations with their peers.
				• Children challenge themselves to solve problems by taking risks in their learning, trying out new and more difficult activities.
				
				• Children are open to sharing understanding so that misconceptions can be effectively solved.
				
				• There is a calm, purposeful, learning atmosphere in which children develop self-esteem and confidence.

Evidence

How well are children helped to make a positive contribution to the provision and their community?

Factors to evaluate	Emerging	Evolving	Establishing	Enhancing

How practitioners support children to behave appropriately through routines.
 	
EYFS themes
 	
  A Unique Child
 	
  Positive Relationships
	• Children are supported to understand that there are boundaries and rules.
	
	• Policies on behaviour take into account the needs and ages of the children.
	
	• Practitioners model a range of positive behaviours.
		• There is a calm atmosphere with consistent boundaries in which children can develop appropriate behaviour.
		
		• Practitioners model expected patterns of behaviour positively with encouragement.
			• Children display evidence of positive relationships with their peers.
			
			• Children are able to work together to solve personal problems.
				• Children and adults have positive, trusting relationships.
				
				• Children are able to negotiate conflict resolution when working in teams.
				
				• Adults have training in conflict resolution.

Evidence

Valuing Quality in the Early Years © Carmen Mohamed and Sarah Lissaman

Factors to evaluate	Emerging	Evolving	Establishing	Enhancing

The extent to which practitioners ensure that children feel they belong in the setting.
 	
EYFS themes
 	
  A Unique Child
 	
  Positive Relationships
	• Children have a place to put their belongings.
	
	• They see their work displayed.
	
	• Children are encouraged to share stories that are important to them.
	
	• Children know who to go to when they need comfort or support.
		• All children's achievements are celebrated.
		
		• Displays and activities evidence a value of home culture and family make up.
		
		• All children have equal access to activities and can engage with them successfully.
			• An ethos is established in which individual achievements and backgrounds are valued.
			
			• Children are encouraged to use their home language.
			
			• Experiences reflect children's developing interests and the cultural diversity of society.
				• Children are protected against early failure.
				
				• They know they can take risks, feeling confident and secure in their explorations.
				
				• Children's self-confidence and a positive attitude towards themselves and others is promoted whatever their background or needs.

Evidence

How well are children helped to make a positive contribution to the provision and their community?

Factors to evaluate	Emerging	Evolving	Establishing	Enhancing
How practitioners work alongside parents for the benefit of the children. **EYFS themes** *Positive Relationships* *Enabling Environments*	• There are regular recorded discussions with parents about how well their child is settling in to the new environment. • Parents know what opportunities for play the children have accessed through the session. • Children are encouraged to bring favourite stories or toys from home to the setting. • Key workers sensitively approach parents whose children are having difficulty settling into the new routines.	• Trust and respect for parents and children is evident in contact. • Practitioners develop their work with parents, carers and the wider community through regular contact and events. • Parents know what opportunities for learning the children have experienced. • Parents are offered suggestions for working with their child at home.	• Parents are asked for their opinion about how the setting is run and they know they are listened to. • Parents are encouraged to be involved in their children's learning at home and share their observations with the key workers. • Story, rhyme and maths sacks are offered for parents to take home and share with their children.	• Parents are seen as primary educators of their children. • Parents welcome other parents to the setting. • Sessions to support parental understanding of how their children are learning are regularly held. • Discussion and documentation of children's learning and development is a two-way process. • Parents are invited to 'Family Learning Trails', activity sessions or fun days.

Evidence

Factors to evaluate	Emerging	Evolving	Establishing	Enhancing
The extent to which practitioners use the community and local environment to enrich curriculum experiences. **EYFS themes** *Enabling Environments* *Learning and Development*	• Topics about people who help us include local agencies visiting to talk with the children about their jobs. • Children are taken out of the setting to walk around and talk about the local amenities.	• The local environment is used as a resource when planning topics. • Children are taken out to the locality on walking trips, for example nature and sound walks and the local library.	• The local environment is regularly used as a resource when planning learning experiences. • Children visit the locality on a variety of appropriately focused trips to enhance their learning.	• The local environment is consistently used as a natural resource when planning for children's learning. • Children are encouraged to learn about the world around them through real-life experience. • Parents, carers and members of the local community are regular visitors who share their jobs and interests with the children.

Evidence

How well is the setting organised and managed?

Factors to evaluate	Emerging	Evolving	Establishing	Enhancing

Practitioners have a working knowledge of the statutory Early Years Foundation Stage Framework and guidance.
 	
EYFS themes
   Enabling Environments
   Learning and Development
   A Unique Child
   Positive relationships
	• The EYFS guidance is used to support planning and assessment of children's development and learning.
	
	• Curriculum requirements are understood and are implemented effectively.
		• There is provision for different starting points from which individual children develop their learning.
		
		• Relevant and appropriate content and resources match children's needs.
		
		• Activities are provided both indoors and outdoors.
		
		• Principles of the guidance are developed and are in evidence.
			• Children develop purposeful learning experiences from different starting points.
			
			• Relevant and appropriate experiences are driven by the children's needs.
			
			• Carefully planned and purposeful experiences are consistently in evidence both indoors and outdoors.
				• Practitioners are committed, enthusiastic and reflective with a breadth of knowledge, skills and understanding of how young children learn.
				
				• This is evident in interventions, questioning and explaining to extend and challenge children's development and learning.
				
				• Planning is flexible and responsive to observation of children's development.

Evidence

Valuing Quality in the Early Years © Carmen Mohamed and Sarah Lissaman

Factors to evaluate	Emerging	Evolving	Establishing	Enhancing
The clarity of vision and direction of the management. **EYFS themes** *A Unique Child* *Enabling Environments* *Learning and Development* *Positive relationships*	• An action plan for the development of provision in line with requirements for Early Years Foundation Stage is in place. • Funding is provided for consumables.	• The development plan is regularly evaluated and progress is monitored through action planning. • Action plans are clear, focused and manageable. • Budgets are informed by the needs of young children.	• Action is taken to develop specific areas of the environment, with clearly focused expectations for success of strategy in terms of impact on children. • Budgets are informed by the learning needs of young children.	• Monitoring systems help to improve practice and provision. • Practitioners demonstrate the capability and capacity to improve all aspects of provision. • Leadership has vision and direction and is responsive to new initiatives. • Value for money is ensured.

Evidence

How well is the setting organised and managed?

Factors to evaluate	Emerging	Evolving	Establishing	Enhancing
The effectiveness of policies and procedures. **EYFS themes** *A Unique Child* *Positive Relationships* *Learning and Development* *Enabling Environment*	• Policies and procedures are in line with requirements for Early Years Foundation Stage. • Parents are made aware of policies and procedures; they are accessible and explained. • Guidance on recording and reporting of information is followed accurately.	• All staff are involved in regular review and evaluation of policies and procedures. • Parents are consulted in the writing of new policies and procedures; these are made available if requested. • Recording and reporting of information supports children's learning and development.	• All staff regularly review and evaluate policies and procedures to ensure they are obvious in practice. • Parents are consulted when policies are written, evaluated in practice or when reviewed. • Recording and reporting of information is systematic and enhances provision for children's learning and development.	• Staff have a shared philosophy about how the setting should support the children. This is discussed and written into policy and procedure for all to follow. • Parents are involved in writing policies and procedures. • Parents are actively involved in discussion about changes in policies and procedures. • Recording and reporting of information is rigorous and is instrumental in children's development and well being.

Evidence

Factors to evaluate	Emerging	Evolving	Establishing	Enhancing
The range of qualifications and training, alongside continuous professional development. **EYFS themes** *A Unique Child* *Positive Relationships* *Learning and Development* *Enabling Environment*	● Minimum standards for qualifications and ratios are met. ● Practitioners take part in regular training events and meetings to stay informed about developments. ● There is a system of appraisals which informs training needs.	● Minimum standards for qualifications and ratios are surpassed. ● A continuous cycle of training and development is linked to the needs of the children and the setting. ● Managers consistently evaluate practice, recognising the importance of identifying and meeting training needs. ● Regular appraisal informs professional development.	● All practitioners are qualified to the highest level. ● Further learning and qualifications enhance the quality of the setting and result in constructive outcomes. ● Managers and leaders cascade training information and make appropriate changes to the setting. ● There is a regular cycle of appraisals which culminates in a staff training plan.	● Team Leader has L6/EYPS qualification. ● Action research is undertaken within the setting to ensure highest quality experiences for the children. ● Team members use each other as a critical friend to support their own development, including peer observations. ● There is a regular system of appraisals which informs career development.

Evidence

How well is the setting organised and managed?

Factors to evaluate	Emerging	Evolving	Establishing	Enhancing
Staff and resources are effectively deployed to support children's care and development. **EYFS themes** **A Unique Child** **Positive Relationships** **Learning and Development** **Enabling Environment**	• There are adequate resources to support learning across all areas of development. • All staff are well informed about requirements for Early Years Foundation Stage care and education.	• All practitioners contribute to planning, teaching and assessment. • All staff have a consistent approach to working with young children.	• All staff are well informed about current Early Years issues. • Responsibilities for all aspects of the setting are shared amongst all staff. • All staff have high expectations of children's achievements and well being.	• Constructive insights and evidence from review and evaluation is acted upon quickly. • All staff are critically reflective and self-evaluative; this is demonstrated in the quality of provision.

Evidence

Factors to evaluate	Emerging	Evolving	Establishing	Enhancing
Comprehensive links to ensure smooth transition and continuity. **EYFS themes** *A Unique Child* *Positive Relationships* *Learning and Development* *Enabling Environment*	• Links are put in place at times of transition so that children and receiving practitioners have some contact prior to movement. • Links are developed between all settings any child attends.	• Parents are seen as partners in information sharing about the child. • Practitioners develop links with partner settings to support the children. • There is regular sharing of information between partner settings.	• Children and parents share experiences and information with receiving settings. • Practitioners develop strong, supportive links with partner settings. • There are regular discussions around shared curriculum provision to ensure continuity of experiences.	• Parents are included as partners in information and experience sharing. • There are regular visits throughout the year to and from partner settings. • Children and their parents are familiar with staff from each stage of the transition.

Evidence

Factors to evaluate	Emerging	Evolving	Establishing	Enhancing
The effectiveness of records of achievement in enhancing children's progress. **EYFS themes** *A Unique Child* *Positive Relationships* *Learning and Development* *Enabling Environment*	• Profiles of the children's developmental achievements are collated over time and passed on to relevant bodies. • Profiles are moderated within the setting.	• Accurate profiles of the children's developmental achievements are collated and tracked over time to monitor areas for development. • Information gathered through profiling is used to develop appropriate learning opportunities. • Profiles are regularly moderated within the setting.	• Profiles and documented Learning Journeys of the children's achievements are used in the target-setting process to enable tracking of progress. • Quality data is used to enhance learning opportunities. • Profiles are routinely moderated within and from outside the setting.	• Records show the children achieve challenging targets and take account of trends over time, including any significant variations between groups of learners. • Quality data drives change and development within the setting. • All aspects of the child's development are considered when making assessments, recording Learning Journeys or analysing data to define next steps.

Evidence

Targets	Action (How it will be done. Who is involved? Who is leading?)	Resources (People and budget.)	Time scales (Start date and estimated finish time.)	Monitoring and evaluation (Who and how?)

References

The Creative Teaching and Learning Toolkit by Brin Best and Will Thomas (Continuum International Publishing Group 2007)

The Early Years Foundation Stage: setting the standards for learning, development and care for children from birth to five. DCSF. 2007

Key Elements of Effective Practice. Primary National Strategy DfES. 2005

Further suggested reading

The Thinking Child: Brain-based learning for the Foundation Stage by Nicola Call and Sally Featherstone (Network Educational Press Ltd. 2004)

The Thinking Child Resource Book by Nicola Call and Sally Featherstone (Network Educational Press Ltd. 2006)

Coaching Solutions Resource Book by Will Thomas (Network Educational Press Ltd. 2005)

Nature's Playground by Danks and Jo Scholfield (J. Frances Lincoln Ltd. 2005)

Learning Outdoors: Improving the quality of young children's play outdoors. Edited by Helen Bilton (David Fulton. 2005)

Because We're Worth It: Enhancing Self-Esteem in Young Children by Margaret Collins (Lucky Duck Publishing Ltd. 2001)

Foundation Stage Audit Materials (Teacher Training Agency, now TDA. 2004)

Quality in Diversity in Early Learning (NCB 1998)

Effective Early Learning Project (Worcester College of Higher Education, directed by Professor Christine Pascall. 1995)

Suggested websites

www.singup.org

www.bongoclub.org.uk

www.talktoyourbaby.org.uk

www.ican.org.uk

www.ltl.org.uk

www.forestschools.com

www.ncb.org.uk